The Hunger in Plain View

Selected Poems

Ester Naomi Perquin

Selected and translated by
David Colmer

WHITE PINE PRESS / BUFFALO, NEW YORK

White Pine Press
PO Box 236
Buffalo, NY 14201

www.whitepine.org

This translation is published with the permission of the Dutch publisher Uitgeverij G.A. van Oorschot b.v.

Acknowledgments: Some of these translations have been published previously by *Plume, Five Dials, Little Star, Cordite Review, Dutch Magazine,* and *Poetry International.*

Publication of this book was made possible, in part, by the Dutch Foundation for Literature; public funds from the New York State Council on the Arts with the support of Governor Andrew M. Cuomo and the New York State Legislature, a State Agency; and with funds from the National Endowment for the Arts, which believes that a great nation deserves great art.

Cover photograph: Matt Weibe

ISBN 978-1-945680-05-2

Library of Congress number 2016949220

The Hunger in Plain View

Contents

from *Celinspecties* (Cell Inspections) 2012

New Work

from

Napkins at Half-Mast (2007)

Convert

At home in the hinterland I knew
ill-considered quantities, dolloped
excess from pans and bowls.

In the morning when they were still asleep
you could paint a cross on their backs
and eat them come evening.

But here they don't want to know about steel
or stabbing, no one comes for those
who wake up warm and healthy.

Only what grows from one's own earth
belongs on the plate, the knife serves
to determine the direction of the forks,

not to draw through a throat
not to scrape over bones
that are also our bones.

Here they eat at bare-wood tables.
I drink their homemade wine, listen
to sounds from unmolested coops.

Here the white flags flutter.
At home, after every meal,
we flew the napkins at half-mast.

Wanted

Man with big hands and ditto bookcase,
a sea view if possible.

Excessive smoking allowed, along with watching movies
I already know the end of.

Promises for later preferably insincere
so that his stories can always be explained

like pants that are too short,
a man who always fits,

who will learn to love me but
remains unreasonable and packs a punch,

university educated, then unexpectedly
wants me to have his kids.

Reincarnation

Will someone want to walk in my legs,
put words they've chosen in my mouth
or smooth stiff fingers limber in my hands
to play piano or caress someone—
who'll want to put me on?

Will I be first choice or were
the beautiful bodies all too tight?
Will I be folded in the storeroom
or draped on display in the window?

How will they know my me?
Which label, invisible for now,
has been sewn into my neck?

Winter

Let this winter pass into another winter.
No more stately brooding. No bluebird's eggs.
No driven mating or well-built nests.
I want the frost to blast the ground forever
with every seed or shoot that it conceals.

Leave streets as gray as winter has them.
The muddy slush of butchered days,
two blue mittens where the ice was thin.
The lambs are more than I can take.

Nothing worse than the rank excess
of spring exploding into growth.
Below it ice is silencing a son.

Amid this life, he doesn't count.
No sunlight strong enough to draw him up.

No springtime longs to seek him out.

Field Trip

"Duck down under the windows, kids,
we're almost back at school, they'll think,
you've all gone up in smoke."

Someone pushed me into the dark between two seats,
Flat against the stinking wall, I saw
a stream of candy wrappers in apple juice
go trickling round those forty shoes.

Was I the lostest of the class?
I thought I'd disappeared—
even when the rest leaped up
and screamed as in a single voice—

and cried when after years and years,
my angry father found me.

Girls

So nimble in their everyday chatter,
resting side by side, a row of youthful skin
and silky hair in sun that's much too hot already.

Beach grass tickles legs and freshly-
minted laughter tinkles up to make
the gulls swing overhead in fright.

Untouched from head to toe, they lie
and talk in one and the same voice.
about one and the same mother.

Somehow their essence is the sum
of the eternities inside them all. This quiet
sunlit sharing of age, a body, suntan lotion.

But across the sand a strange
and growing growl that seems to swell
soon sends a shiver through the row.

Like giant breakers rolling in,
boys on implacable bikes
come closer every second.

Neighbor

Yeah her across the road had two boyfriends on the go at once
so you'd see him peering through the curtains at number ten 'cause
he never wants to miss a thing now his wife has got that leg and
their daughter who lives upstairs never lifts a finger though that
son-in-law is nice enough too nice really but hardly ever home
no wonder the drunk from next door tries his hand now and then
and the Christian lady from number seven ticks him off
even if everybody admit it now worships in their own way
that's what the nice gay boy from number three said the other day
when we were standing there with that guy with the dogs
that belong to the lady from number four who can't have kids
because of her plumbing but God you know me I always say
you're better off just keeping it to yourself—

Full Moon

I see him in his bathroom,
silhouetted in the window.
Hard at work in that cramped space,

he smears soap over his jaws,
then takes a razor to slice
the wolf off his face.

Enclosed

Being alone in the sense
of constantly your own smell,
over the wall a view
of unfinished sheds,
cars rusting in a front yard.
The gray of your skin.

But the perfect company
of a wallpapered cell, clippings

of glossy sluts, mothers
breastier than ever, girls
climbing onto laps, daughters

who feed the ducks.

Regarding the Lover

You could stay.
Tomorrow, for instance,
would be a good day to stay.
It will be sunny and we

could play rainy.
A coffee under the covers,
a soft-boiled egg or a plate
with salmon and music

or nothing: only a hunger for,
a longing for, and questions.
But you could also go.
For instance, today.

Attempt

Sheets stripped, bed demolished one slat
at a time, pillows shaken out, somebody
paid to make the red walls gray,

crawled across the wooden floor, found
countless hairs, a burnt match, two buttons.
A piece of torn letter behind the baseboard.

The loose plank nailed down,
windows opened wide, ceiling painted white,
the calendar disembarrassed of its days.

Nothing has happened.
I am teaching memory self-acceptance
through all these things that know you exist.

Beached

It still hasn't been identified,
the animal that lay here yesterday
wings spread on the sand,
body too big almost for the day

but it lay on its side like a horse of
insane proportions, drawn to the coast,
a head like a house, skin smooth
as a toad's or an adder's, eyes
almost grieving, even when closed.

It lay here in the northern light
and deep into the night we stroked its hide
to later sleep through restless, clueless dreams.

Now the talk is all of Gods
and fables--and where it's gone is known by none.

Strange tracks lead into the sea.

from

In the Name of the Other (2009)

Risk Taking

Our usual room. Entirely as agreed the walls erect themselves. The
window unfolds, complete

with drawn curtains. It could be the start of the night or the end
of the day. Permanent twilight,

jokes about the light of day and how there's less and less it bears.
The smell of wood and over-ripe mandarins.

Look, the bed-side cabinets are emerging, the double bed is growing
visible with sheets and blankets,

the bedspread with the stain where he lay. Once downstairs we
recompose our faces, pull up chairs

and the view fills the window: farmland, three unsteady trees.
Long since decided what we'll have now:

the starter that invariably disappoints, the steak and the apple pie.
We are older now and could

afford something better. It rains here most days of the year. The
greatest danger tucks us in

to this same place, this same room, where we hazard our habits,
where we love each other. Again.

Quiz

Do you like to rest in the day and make a man happy at night?
Does the idea of lavender make you feel dejected?
Have you ever considered a hotel?

Cross out: I am not a woman / I am a stupid woman.
In recent years there are at least six things
I have regretted. On my fingertips, I prefer:
gold leaf, paint, tomato juice.

You fit in a suitcase. If you do not fit in a suitcase,
how would you describe yourself? How long
have you been overweight? How often?

If jumping off a bridge, you would still attempt to:
A) point yourself out on a map
B) drift further and further off course
C) turn back halfway

Imagine your disease is an animal. For the healthy, this question
counts double. Which animal would you rather your disease is not?
NB: include the bad days.

Are you more afraid of the result than before?
Write down who you think is asking the questions.

The Last Stranger

So you lived secretly, born underground,
never in the picture.

So you lived in places onlookers never frequented,
where abandoned dogs never wandered, noses close to the ground,
you were never tempted to caress somebody
in clear view.

You did not utter any well-written words,
had no meticulous face—how,
if we did not see you, did you live?

Were you hiding from someone somewhere?
Did it seem like the other way round to you—were we lost
as long as you had no truck with us?

You can no longer leave the way you came,
in the dark, like a secret. Stay sitting there
while we zoom in.

This is your chance to be present.

You Are the Wrong Man

You always were the wrong man
and you, incontrovertibly, are the wrong man still.

I don't like love and never have.
I've stayed with you because I am so sure of it.

All that staring into someone else's eyes, someone
         non-interchangeable,
who always has to do something, to go away, to move.

With you I knew from day one
that it wouldn't work, that after a couple of evenings
of well-intentioned conversation, fumbling by full moon,
it would stop. And it did.

(It stopped, it kept stopping, less dangerous
by the day, more indifferent, more tenacious.)

Someone else, that's: Paris, real life,
nights, the people in ads, hell.

Maybe I do love you, as long as I don't stop
meaning it as something inalienable,
as long as I can keep it safe and well.

Example

You can do it all in a single day: fall in love with a man,
pat yourself on and knife yourself in the back, think
about the whiteness of your teeth, study your face
as if you're him, looking up and seeing you.

You can find yourself ugly or not and ask yourself out
(kissing somewhere, staying sober at the same time),
be indulgent about routes you come up with
—where he lives, works, where he drinks—
have a word to yourself concerning possible,
yet to be formed indifference.

You can regret the day with the man
with the regret you fell in love with.

You can think: there is no alternative,
reduced to a single day of this
perjured eternity.

***

This morning a lady phoned wanting to know if I
was Richard. This had never happened before.

Many people have wished I was someone, sometimes someone
I was in the past, sometimes someone I should become—look
scared for a change, talk like a nun, jump up and down,
can't you wear a skirt for once—but
nobody's asked me to be Richard.

(Meanwhile the silence on two sides is murmuring in my ear.)

Until I answer there is another life, crammed with possibility,
the material I am made up of could just as easily have had
a different name or shape. What if I said, Yes,
yes, it's me, Richard. Is that you, Mom?
It's been so long.

Would becoming Richard make me Richard, including his body,
breath, secrets, the way he ties his laces in the morning?
Does he like parsnips, for instance?

Would his mother hang up or would she,
in her persistence
or out of friendliness
or loneliness,
believe me?

Is Richard still alive or does she always phone someone else,
asking for him because who knows maybe someone
will say, Richard? Sure. He's upstairs.

Don't let anyone tell her that Richard drowned, that he's lost
or been kidnapped or killed in a crash. Wasn't there a party
somewhere, a man? Did I not only know Richard
but also kiss him, talk to him, drink his wine,
didn't we laugh together?

Now, right now, it is still possible to not make a sound,
to hang up or start crackling bags as if we—unfortunately—
are snowed in, I can't hear you.

I imagine her standing in a dark room, a quizzical look on her face.
But what about me? Where do I find a Richard at this hour?

I'm sorry, honesty compels me to tell you
that I am not Richard, never have been,
I don't have a clue, and though our numbers
may vary only slightly, our lives are separated
by an eight, a four, a two.

There are people who differ less than one digit from me
but their mothers don't know me, wouldn't call me.

You're wasting your time, I'm only made up of half voices,
half faces, not worthy of a Richard, I never gave
anyone more than half-hearted presence.

(I hear determined silence on the line.)

Listen, I don't know who to, but I'll pray with you
that someone will succeed.

That someone will succeed in being Richard.

Guard Duty

At night the ex-prison guard's wife
hears the sliding bolts and cannot sleep.

A man stays true to place longer than he knows,
cells are reconstructed in his deepest breath
and with him close like this she hears
the convicts walking circles in his head.

She listens in on hurried conversations: break lurk,
mulligan, blood tub, on the shallow.
She keeps her eyes peeled—

sometimes one climbs the wall, slides
through sheets, gets out of his skull.

Strangers

Like the way you see yourself in a photo taken from behind
but would rather not be that person because
it's so unnatural—the other

is just like you thought: it's not good to know too much,
secrets show intelligence, give you something to do.

Dig a sea between yourself / the other and soak your hair in dye,
lay silence over all attempts to reconcile,
resist approaches with rigid names and titles.

Refuse to hush up anything and go to war,
be immutable always. Never coincide.

Older Brother

No dad or mom to order us down from the trees
for bed or supper, the best climbing summer for years.

I refused a ponytail, ripped dresses to shreds,
got my hair caught on branches—you fetched
scissors and I became a soldier but
the sword was so heavy and
I could not lift the shield.

You yelled me higher—so I climbed and climbed.
The heat hung in the trees till late at night with
you, lying like an animal on the lowest bough.

No lions or murderers could come upon us.
I was—for a girl—an excellent lookout.

Sign Here, Please

They came for the others at night in cars with dark windows.
For you they came, surprised themselves, in broad daylight.

Like a dignified host, dinner ready, top hat on your head,
you went straight up to them. Ah, gentlemen, you recognize me,
of course, you have the incontestable date in your pocket

and they must have thought: this can't be the right one,
this man is not real, he's bound to have a woman in a
feather skirt hidden somewhere, a dove up his sleeve,

he laughs like a king, he bows like a servant, soon
he'll conjure up some rabbits, it'll all be a joke;
we were evidently expected here and that too

is something we cannot accept, in full view like this,
half the city arrayed before the gate—

but you took the unforgiving documents from their hands,
smiled for a moment and then carefully
put a cross beside the name and date.

f

from

Cell Inspections (2012)

***

That day I tumbled, unsuspecting, into someone else's life,
someone else's driving lesson, shopping list,
lecture, into someone else's hesitations,
beginner's legs at ballet.

And nowhere was I lost, I walked countless orphans
to respectable parents and taught a drinking man
to trust his glass would last,

I stormed bruised and battered women out of houses,
shuffled beggars into castles, made a cold mother
kneel in time beside a fallen child,
I was that fallen child.

I taught a soccer player to believe in God like the smack
of the ball on the crossbar, a blind man to find
everything he lacked without asking,
I was the talent the painter had
to rise above his light.

Only a skinny, early-morning swimmer's
totally unquestioning dive into
the pool between the trees,
came out too forced.

Powerless, she hovered over the water while I slipped back,
in motion once again, leaving her to shiver, losing heart,
the swimsuit already starting
to vanish.

Within Limitations

You get used to your format. Walls built up out of patience, the height of the ceiling with peculiar stains, a sticky floor, your unstoppable breath feels out the room and rebounds, in the dark your hands know where to find the switch, your cigarettes, know how to move, you get used to smoking in the dark, the visions of your sons still the most intense, them riding round on bikes with flat tires, wielding tools nobody explains, drawing a bead on the wrong birds, scraping their cheeks raw with your blunt razor. You get used to it. Under the blankets your wife tosses and turns herself naked, you feel her next to you, stretched out life-size, and try to touch her, you get used to a body nobody ever caresses and more and more lost, you circle her, difficult to console. You get used to the view like you get used to a story, the one who read it to you, almost asleep, years ago now, the point mostly escaped you, and it's not the only thing you've forgotten and you get used to the afterimage that is left: thieves leap out and start singing, and there's a man with a scythe, a woman in a tower, arms spread as if waiting to fall but she's waiting of her own free will, smiling. You get used to it. There being some intrepid someone who will later come to rescue her, defeating the thieves and mowing down the man with the scythe. You get used to the tendency to call her in. To remaining hesitant at first, then your habits, a stripe of light on the sheets, the iron door, the leaking faucet, the cigarette burns in the curtains, your nude and accommodating posters, the all-seeing head that bends at night, the breath of justice, other men talking and distant music, the way things start to creak, the slow departure of steps down the corridor, you get used to being afraid, your complete nakedness, sperm on your hand, slug that you are, you get used to turning things over, to the pointless breathless never-ending constant, you get used to the constant thinking.

Statement

I wasn't there that night. And if I was, I didn't know. Not
that they were drinking, you hear things sometimes,
it's only now I realize they did something wrong.

I had no idea what was going on, anyway everyone
I saw there left me out of it because
I wasn't there. Not that night.

As far as that woman goes, I wouldn't know. I never
knew her and if I'd known her I wouldn't have
thought about her much because if a woman's
a friend's, you forget her.

You forget your friends too, those guys, for instance. I've never seen
them before and, because I don't know who they are,
I don't know where they were that night.

But things just happen at your place and mine,
in the homes of complete strangers, things
happen in places you've never been to.

Maybe it was a planter. And that planter fell
horizontally on her face and fairly hard and
maybe more than once perhaps but
people talk so much, it was a
remarkably dark night.

I remember I was home in bed where
I was and looking out and thinking
it's not often you see such
a deep black.

***

I can only tell this story once. The second time will sound rehearsed
and round here they're not so keen on stories that sound as if
you've given them a lot of thought, they want them blurted
and bleeding from your lips, like something happening
here and now before their eyes.

I can only tell this story once and that's a lot more difficult
than I'd have guessed. It seems that guilty consciences
really do exist—who'd have thought it—but I
could also say: it's modesty.

I can only tell this story once and that's why I'm going to tell it
exactly like it happened in real life, in other words, including
certain people not knowing anything about it at all.

I can only tell this story once, that's why I want to tell it properly
right away. That's why I'm telling it to you.

This is the story. The story starts now.

Carlo "the Conqueror" da C.

Them catching me; it can't have been the loot. I didn't keep a thing
and I definitely didn't live off it. I didn't have any fences. I wasn't
one of those sad, hungry thieves in search of goods.

Watchful, yeah. I always see an opening, a gap
where no-one sees a chink. I deploy character.

Say there's a house, raised up out of iron and concrete, six guards,
access roads blocked; I got in. I didn't take a thing, no treasure,
no souvenirs—that bothered the old judge, the kind of man
who never sees the beauty of anything, of rooms strangers
never enter—he just went on about what was there
for the taking—as if I hadn't noticed.

I don't need their TV. What was there for the taking I've still got.
They can't confiscate a single inch of all the distances I've won,
all the rooms I've seen and every roof I climbed
so I could stand and be the king.

***

You can also think it's someone else's fault, all of it, because
there's always a choice, everyone is always a maker of choices.
Everyone is always a maker.

You can grab a bike if your bike has been stolen,
not out of vengeance, but out of justice.

You can put off confession till the murder's
been buried: scot-free, cold case.

You can also remember who you liked, if you
liked somebody. There is always a choice,
everyone is always a maker of choices.

You can let a boy grow up until
he no long looks like a boy
and call him a man.

Letters to a P.O. Box

First you need to learn to write to a woman (a letter
that will be seen by strangers, held up to the light),
a woman who will lick her lips between your lines,
clean up that jail-worn body,
patch it.

Whatever you were before, she writes, it doesn't count,
it was in vain, I wasn't there—

Then when you get her in your hands, you have to be bright
and cheerful and fit into her spotless house. Get used
to cushions on the couch, tablecloths, little china
dogs, smoking outside and special bowls
for soup, her mother's face, apple pie,
the photo on the sideboard,
that face leering at you.

You are so clean-shaven, freshly-showered, strong and silent,
she says, and then you kiss her. You never say a word.
Your childhood alone would stain her rugs.

Nothing Happened

There were all kinds of reasons to have a kid,
so we had a kid. He was a boy,
big for his age, quiet.

We bought a house and had two daughters
because an only child, quiet, is too sad.

There were marauders on the prowl.
We bought a dog with sharp fangs
because a house needs guarding,
preferably day and night.

We went on vacation with three kids,
the dog and thoughts of the house,
meanwhile defenseless, abandoned,
We sent it picture postcards
from the beach.

David H.

Because I knew her face much better than she knew mine—
I made her disappear a little bit at first, then more and more
until I too was no longer sure where she'd gone to—

because I had studied her much more carefully than she had
studied me and because I understood more about us,
because her face is often so clear in my mind,
I sometimes wonder if she would have seen
me at all if I hadn't asked her something.
If she would have existed if I
had let her drive on.

Of course it was love—but love can't lie, it doesn't scream
when you say, quiet, it doesn't run out of breath and
doesn't force me into anything. Love lies down
before you and listens. True love
is always willing.

As far as that goes, I know better now. I wouldn't have looked
at her like that, I would have loved her differently,
not in a hurry with my two hands round her neck,
but thoughtfully, mournfully, gently.

Delay

We are modern. It's the wrong century for love and there
are no women anywhere standing on towers
looking out. The last knight
died of syphilis.

We have lost the knack of fluttering banners,
the whispering between the stones,
song and the names of flowers.

Hastily we toss each other
body parts in passing.
All is well.

Bolt the doors when it grows dark.
Stay here with me.
Lock your horse.

About Us

Of all the things they taught us in that place—how to stand tall
in a headwind, buy a suit, do up a necktie, save money,
how to shape your voice to a clean conscience, walk
away, hold tight, how to wait, talk to women,
eat politely—not much remained.

We were incorrigibly made to rob and break, with hands like big
purposeful scoops, eyes like holes, teeth that can bite through
steel, with well-hatched plans, a pitch-black past,
brains bent to a life in the gutter. Our cant
is full of bullets, disease and body parts.

There Is a Lot Left

You can leave birds that have been hit by a car, you can
push them aside still flapping, easily forgotten

a bike that falls over in the rain, used needles in a sandpit,
strategically located banana peel, unmailed letters
to internal revenue oblige you to nothing

excess change in your hand, a small boy on a bus
who doesn't know where to get off, you can ignore coolly,
not recognizing faces, not acknowledging a smile

it is completely legal to turn your back
on dumbstruck former classmates
anxious to chat in a busy store

and your hand, you can turn that into a weapon,
stick it in your pocket. Sawed-off. Cocked.

Dennis de K.

Am I supposed to start writing about my childhood, am I supposed
to explain my parents from in here, people like that,
their mugs aren't going to come as any surprise—

so what do you want? Boozehounds, of course, and blows,
lashes from my father's belt, my mother floored
and was I crying or not, did I know about it?

Am I supposed to vomit the whole mess up in writing? All those
movies you know with guys like me when they're little,
thin pajamas, soft lighting and those books and photos,
sharp-sketched Bambi anecdotes, never before
put into such throat-choking,
tear-gulping words—

Take it from me: I never learned how
to move others. I'm eighteen.
Locked up for murder.

You want me to write down my life, string those people up
and forget about all the other
mindfuckers—

And even if I hold my pig-headed tongue, you know.
Thousands of other guys did it better.

So to Speak

Anyway now you're here, I wrote you letters and never
mailed them, learned your number off by heart
and mumbled it aimlessly to myself,
gradually taking your existence
personally.

I rented a house on the shore and had your name
engraved alongside mine on a brass plate.
Such well-matched initials, the man said.
An auspicious sign.

No need for you to pay that any mind of course.
It's not as if I'm going to turn up naked
late one night to put on a show,
don't think that.

But with things between us going so well
I thought it would be nice if you
were in on it too.
That's why.

Fathers, Sons

He still came home but that coming was imbued with signs
of resistance—more, we thought, for the bed
and food than us, not to be home.

After a glance he seemed to forget us completely, stalking
backache-stiff to the cabinet, pouring a drink and
packing himself away, as it were, disappearing.

We always wanted him to tell us which of us was tallest
that day, who had the broadest shoulders,
who was best at chess.

He was never alone—while he ignored us we managed
to reveal him bit by bit, increasing his importance
one question at a time.

At night when we went to bed he got scared, came up to our room
and stood there staring—dragging the laurels down
further on his wounded brow.

Confessions

I.

Sometimes I watched their movements from above, standing
on the edge of the world and counting their circuits
of the square, their progress, their numb
mandatory walking, and I rewound them.

I rewound them and they shrank. Their printed T-shirts
became as vast as sheets, their unshaven jaws grew
soft, their jutting hips swiveled back, teeth
disappeared, gold slipped down.

Lying there looking at the sky for the first time, they waved
their little hands in front of their eyes, invented sounds,
gazed vacantly at birds, vacantly at trees.

Sometimes I'd write cards. The joy, the name and date.
The exact weight of the son.

So alone and all those troubles still to come.
Crying in desperation.

2.

I only wanted to touch men who were bad news. To feel
their shoulders under my hands, unbuttoning them,
quickly getting undressed, wrapping them
around me like blankets, laying myself
to sleep in their arms.

I wanted to carefully wash them, working up a lather with
non-sting shampoo, massaging foam into their skin,
buffing them until they gleamed.

I wanted to give them cars and make little houses for them,
sit them down at a table with a wife, a plate of food,
a kid who says dad, a calico cat.

I wanted to take them into the woods with me, dress them up
warm and send them off in the right direction, where
the trees are so tangled you can't find any paths,
nothing at all, just, when it gets dark,
very realistic, hungry bears.

If You Lose Me

Start by making casual inquiries on the platforms, I love trains,
I like getting lost, ask if anyone's seen me, fill out forms
saying what I'm wearing, what I look like.

Then find a photo—use the one on the beach that flatters
my nose—and pin my face up on countless
corners, in bars I have never been to
(you would stake your life on it).

If it takes too long, if you can't sleep at night without my turning,
sighing or getting up, having to jot down words
to make sure I don't forget them,

if you do sleep but aren't woken by my sudden stuttering
laugh (I was dreaming something I've forgotten,
that faded but was so funny),

you can spend months anxiously asking complete strangers
if they've seen me or spoken to me, and when,
are they sure, what did I say and what did I
keep to myself, was I lying back then—

Afterwards you can slowly forget the color of my hair and eyes,
the way I always swore in German and cooked pasta
to mush, how I could talk for no reason
in the gaps you left

and later still you get over it completely: the way I usually
couldn't wait to let go of your hand when walking
beside you, invariably wanted to stay at parties
for just one more hour and ended up
disappearing too.

Bart V.

There were people who looked at me. A toddler with an ice-cream,
a woman with a bag with leeks sticking out of it. There was a man
who was just pulling his reading glasses out of his pocket
because of a shopping list and afterwards he was still
holding them in his hand.

Later you learn that you have to forget enough to make space
for what is yet to come: there will always be questions
in dark rooms, with flickering lights.

So you push what you know out of view, into unpunished
territory where scholars bicker and squabble. I hear them
thrashing about on paper, exchanging accusations.

There were people who tripped on a step
while running and didn't make the door ,
a girl who cried "Oh, honey."

Oh, honey. She smiled very briefly and then
fell down as if she'd been a coat that had
suddenly slipped off a hanger.

Conversation on the Street

A man speaks, no, he doesn't speak, he screams into his cell phone
who the hell, he takes a breath, he sees me standing there,
who do you think you are

with your so-called manners all your rich friends
your completely-booked-up week your good job
his voice breaks the phone open

the woman rolls out over the street, half dressed, mascara
smudged, scrambles to her feet in shock
and he starts again from the top

who do you think you are and watches me while hitting her,
watching until I shout *enough* stop *she's already curled*
up in a ball she's not hurting you man stop

but he's not finished yet and watches me and asks
who do you think unrelenting forming words
in the palm of his hand *you are*
and doesn't stop again

Michael van W.

No matter what they're after, the dogs inside my head are always
ravenous, always parched. Don't talk about it. The daylight
chases them away, for a while—but as soon as I lie down
the trouble starts, they scratch me awake, whimpering
for bitches or meat, demanding that I let them out.

What name do you give that? Is there a word for the man that I
become when I cut loose and corner an alley cat, do you file it
under madness or murder, will that leash me? They don't listen.
They twist, they threaten—I know them by name, their spots

and snapping jaws—but I don't want to talk about it, not here,
not now it's light. Don't be scared. I feel safe here.
Did you know there's a book with that name?

On the cover there's a man and his mouth—you see him growling,
his teeth—his fangs bared and behind him
the full moon, that hypocritical.

Like him, as hairy as a dog—that's what I'd be if I could.
I'd look like him. Wearing this madness that drives me,
the hunger in plain view.

Legal Activities

1.

Wake them up at the start of the night
and ask for dreams.

If they say they haven't had any yet because
you've woken them up: slap.

If they start to cry, stroke their hair until they think
of their mothers. Then say their mothers
aren't coming anymore.

If they rest their heads on their arms, keep quiet
for a long time. When they fall asleep,
wake them up and ask for dreams.

If they tell you their dreams, listen and explain that things
like that don't exist. Then move on to the order of the day.
Then start again from the beginning.

2.

Put them in the exercise yard and make the sound of a gunshot.
Practice until you can hit a slow pigeon in flight
just over their heads, and have them
bury the pigeon.

Or turn them over onto their backs and draw their outline
on the mattress with a marker and make them
stand up to look at themselves.

Ask them if the outline reminds them
of anyone. Ask them who.

Song

Bennie, of all the things you learned, most were in vain.
You knew that and laughed it off and once again I see
your darting hands, as if you were interpreting for the deaf,

it doesn't help, you said: pulling gloves on over claws. Nails cut
through fingers and leave tracks, deep, five lanes,
claws are claws, you said, they won't stay still.

Look. You showed me your fingers. This is what I have to do. Bite
them off, so short that when I lash out with blood-lust in my heart,
It will be flesh on flesh.

We both knew you weren't like that, Bennie.
You might as well admit it,
you stroked.

You didn't like visitors. The visiting room reminded you of the rooms
where you were questioned, the tables of earlier tables.
The smell of coffee always scared you stiff.

When you got like that, Bennie, they called for me.
I took you to the showers, kept the door ajar
and talked to you through the chink.

Your body still so slight, so thin. A wet dog's eyes. But your mother,
Bennie, your mother's coming. Don't you want to see your mom?
Your mom is here and waiting. We sang a little,
the soap and water calmed you down.

Bennie, you said, has been a naughty boy. In your dreams you still
remembered everything, kept walking through the street
you lived in then and knew the names, you stroked the cats.

All the neighbors' doors were open. They thought you were polite
and gentle. No one saw it coming, that same evening two men
took you away, head bowed with them on either side.
A misunderstanding.

Bennie, you said, went funny in the head. When you dreamed
you didn't want to see and squeezed your eyes shut.
When you were awake, the light had to be on.

You got a stamp in your inch-thick file and I explained
what it was and how it closed the door on you
because no judges saw an opening.

These are my hands, you said, but they don't look like mine.
They're bleeding, but where's the blood coming from?
I haven't cut myself and still it's dripping down.

Take those tablets, Bennie, get some sleep. You have to stay here,
maybe longer than you thought. You know it here.

And don't think we don't want things ourselves, don't think
we get away from the blow with which a stamp
descends on a sheet of paper.

Bennie, there was a lot of talk when you were found
and nobody wanted to think about the last thing
you did, nobody asked any questions.

They didn't blame me, I didn't take it on myself either, the blame lay
there on the table for the taking and lay there still
when we left, it had happened,
we had work to do.

Later the warden called your mother and I was standing there and
got her on the line as well and had it under control
until she said it must be
a sad day for you too.

Nobody asked me what you said that night, nobody thought
about last words, seldom appropriate, usually light
and of a practical bent, I'm going out,
good night, see you later, or I'll call
you back in a while.

But you said, I'd like to save my last breath for home, and I laughed
at your words, I laughed at you, Bennie, for a moment
and locked the door behind you.

New Work

Table Talk

When people talk about people they say "they." They do it
over the starters. You're sitting between them and
nod now and then, but you have no idea
what all the spoons are for.

"They" are other people, not the people who are talking,
but the people they are talking about. I have never
claimed to love the word "they," I just hear it.
I'm no fonder of "it," you think.

"It" is something that happens in another country, in a big drought
with flies everywhere, the smell of fruit not even
describable anymore, all eyes directed at
unreachably distant, fat water birds.

They point out a spelling error in the main course, nudge
each other and laugh, butter their bread. It makes
me think of "a," which is closest to my heart.
A table. A meal. A guinea foul.

When people talk about people they never say, there is someone
here that. Or someone who is clearly. There is definitely,
without doubt, statistically, someone here who.
"They" has excluded us from consideration.

Every dinner has a raped woman. A homosexual.
An illiterate. A man who knows what all
the spoons are for. You're better off
not talking to *him*.

2.

If you have to say something about meat you say "this." This is
the part that has no eyes and no name, that didn't spend days
on end walking around on boggy grass, a bit
you didn't wave at when you were little.

Someone sticks the point of a knife in the back of your hand,
someone attacks you, someone asks for your heart
as if that's something that belongs on the table,
and you decide you'd better make a joke of it.
Nobody laughs.

It's only when you've had too much to drink that you tell the story
of the meat as it really was. You would like to include a farmer
with a double-barreled shotgun, a smoke house full of wood.

But you talk about a screen, a panel with three buttons, the winch,
the advertising man who wanted to make love to his wife
in the middle of the night and then thought
of the perfect slogan.

Brainwaves, you say, are apparently easy to come by when it's right
in front of your nose. When you really bury yourself in it.
Nobody wants to get into that at the moment.

3.

Around the time the last wine has been poured a man gets up
from the table and kneels cautiously beside you.

You can smell what he'll be like later, each evening, when he
has finished his meal, pushes his plate away and looks at you,
you can already guess the words he uses – you look away
and hastily lay your hands on your lap.

In Paris a woman is asked to share her life every minute.
Their existences aren't cramped there, they are
quick to move up, sliding shelves empty
for someone else's things, calling
their mothers with joy.

What you'd like to do now is make an impression. Grabbing
the tablecloth with both hands and whipping it out
in a single movement without knocking
anything over. Everyone clapping.

But the man has laid his head on your knee and
there are gestures you can never escape,
they come to you so naturally.

You stroke his hair, while thinking about
everyone you missed today and how,
vicariously, to touch them.

The Author

Ester Naomi Perquin grew up in the Dutch province of Zeeland but has lived in Rotterdam for most of her adult life. Notably, she put herself through creative writing school by working as a prison guard for four years and draws on this experience often in her work.

Perquin published her first collection of poetry *Napkins at Half-Mast* (2007) at the age of twenty-seven and has published two more collections since: *In the Name of the Other* (2009) and *Cell Inspections* (2012). Her fourth collection, *Multiple Absence,* will be published this year. From 2011 to 2013 she was the poet laureate of Rotterdam. Her poetry has been very well received and she has won prizes for all of her books, including the Netherlands' most prestigious prize for a single collection, the VSB Poetry Prize, for *Cell Inspections*. She is a regular guest at literary festivals in both the Netherlands and abroad.

Besides poetry, Perquin also writes essays, short stories, columns and articles for newspapers and magazines, gives workshops and masterclasses, presents and programs at festivals, and co-hosts a national arts and culture radio show. *The Hunger in Plain View* is her first book in English.

The Translator

David Colmer is an Australian writer and translator who lives in Amsterdam and is specialized in Dutch-language literature—novels and children's books as well as poetry. He has won many translation awards, including major Dutch and Australian prizes for his body of work, the IMPAC-Dublin Literary Award and the Independent Foreign Fiction Prize, both with novelist Gerbrand Bakker. In 2014, *Even Now*, his translation of a selection of the poetry of Hugo Claus, was shortlisted for the PEN Award for Poetry in Translation.

His recent poetry translations include Paul van Ostaijen's *Occupied City*, Menno Wigman's *Window-Cleaner Sees Paintings* and Nachoem M. Wijnberg's *Divan of Ghalib*.

Printed in the USA
CPSIA information can be obtained
at www.ICGtesting.com
JSHW082225140824
68134JS00015B/740

9 781945 680052